WRITE NOW

Doodle
Journal

MY BRILLIANT SCRIBBLES

by

Marigold Dazzle

text by
Karen Phillips

art by
DIRTY BANDITS

KLUTZ

KLUTZ creates activity books and other great stuff for kids ages 3 to 103. We began our corporate life in 1977 in a garage we shared with a Chevrolet Impala. Although we've outgrown that first office, Klutz galactic headquarters remains in Palo Alto, California, and we're still staffed entirely by real human beings. For those of you who collect mission statements, here's ours:

CREATE WONDERFUL THINGS
BE GOOD
HAVE FUN

Write Us We would love to hear your comments regarding this or any of our books. We have many!

KLUTZ
450 Lambert Avenue
Palo Alto, CA 94306

Book printed in Korea. 91
All parts manufactured in Korea.

Distributed in the UK by
Scholastic UK Ltd
Westfield Road
Southam, Warwickshire
England CV47 0RA

Distributed in Australia by
Scholastic Australia Ltd
PO Box 579
Gosford, NSW
Australia 2250

Distributed in Canada by
Scholastic Canada Ltd
604 King Street West
Toronto, Ontario
Canada M5V 1E1

ISBN 978-0-545-39626-4
4 1 5 8 5 7 0 8 8 8

Visit Our Website
You can check out all the stuff we make, find a nearby retailer, request a catalog, sign up for a newsletter, e-mail us, or just goof off!
www.klutz.com

LIGHTEN UP

Some people worry about drawing. They want to do it perfectly. Fortunately, doodles are not drawings. You can't make a mistake in a doodle.

This is a book to fill with your doodles, scribbles, and scrawls. But there's not a lot of white space on these pages.

SO WHERE DO YOU MAKE *your mark*?

ANYWHERE YOU WANT!

The white gel pen shows up bright and clear against any dark color. And doodling **IN** white is about nine times cooler than doodling **ON** white.

SO GET GOING—
doodle white now!

DOODLE AT THE SPEED OF WHITE

The pen that came with this book works best when you doodle at a slow, mellow pace. Work too fast, and the ink might skip. So just relax, breathe deep, and go with the nice, slow flow.

A "mistake" on earth...

...is probably perfect...

4

...on another planet.

Animal Planet

white on!

Don't touch your doodle or turn the page until the ink is dry.

TRULY
MADLY
doodly

Write
or draw
something you
are passionate
about in each
heart...

... and

DECORATE
AS NEEDED
xoxo

M + S

6

Accentuate the NEGATIVE

Artists call the "**B L A N K**" part of a picture the negative space — it's the empty air around an object, or the bare section between colored parts. But these beasties have a little **TOO MUCH** negative space.

Fill in the blanks with **SOLID WHITE** or **STRIPES** or **DOTS** or **SQUIGGLES**...

...or anything you want!

HIGHLIGHTS OF
MY LIFE

You can make anything look shiny just by adding little white highlights.

We got Lacey and Izzy

RAPTOR CAMP

They can be squares

or circles

or tiny diamonds

or anything, really

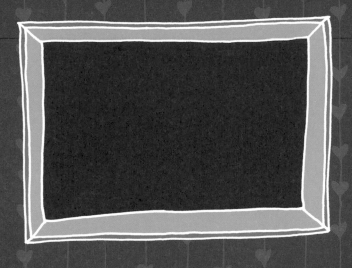

Coincidentally, people also call the best parts of life "highlights."

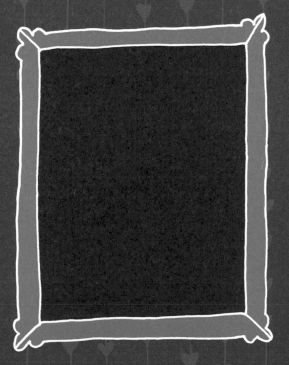

In each of these frames, write one awesome thing that has happened in your life. Then make the frames sparkle with highlights.

What soap is to the body,
laughter is to the soul.
—Yiddish proverb

If you can't get rid of the
skeleton in your closet, you
may as well make it dance.

— George Bernard Shaw

catch some X-rays

If someone had a pair of X-ray goggles and a nosy personality, what would they see in your bag or backpack right now?

Draw or list your answers here.

half a sandwich

phone

sunglasses

unsquishable banana

gym shoes

ALGEBRA

keys to my Ferrari (I wish)

massively heavy math book

lip stuff BALM

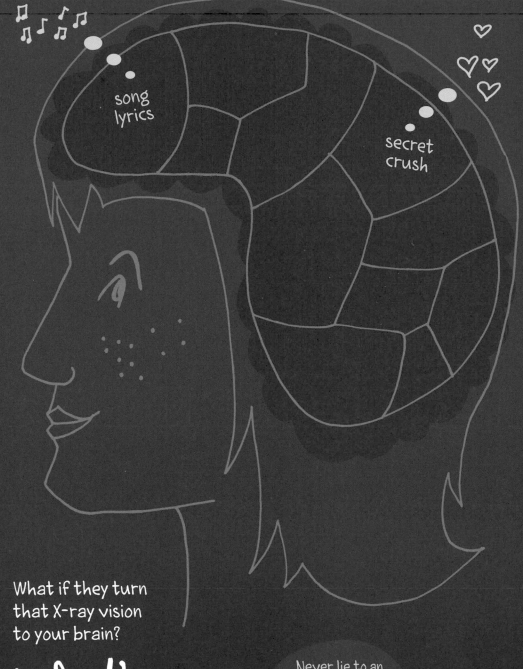

song
lyrics

secret
crush

What if they turn
that X-ray vision
to your brain?

What's
in there?

Never lie to an
X-ray technician.
They can see right
through you.

OOPS

You've heard people say,

It's the craziest
When you noodle
With a doodlin' song.
— Carolyn Leigh

I like the night. Without the dark, we'd never see the stars.
—Stephanie Meyer

What fairy are you?

first name

Which month were you born?

January	Jasmine
February	Violet
March	Daffodil
April	Sweet Pea
May	Primrose
June	Honeysuckle
July	Larkspur
August	Pansy
September	Morning Glory
October	Marigold
November	Chrysanthemum
December	Orchid

second name

What day of the month were you born?

1st – 3rd	Glimmer
4th – 6th	Flicker
7th – 9th	Shimmer
10th – 12th	Wink
13th – 15th	Tickle
16th – 18th	Twinkle
19th – 21st	Dazzle
22nd – 24th	Sparkle
25th – 27th	Glitter
28th – 31st	Glisten

MAGIC

Which color do you love most?

White	snowflakes
Red	strawberries
Orange	flame
Yellow	dandelions
Green	dewdrops
Blue	the moon
Purple	birdsong
Pink	blossoms
Silver	starshine
Gold	sunbeams
Black	cobwebs
EVERY color!	rainbows

I am

Marigold
first name

Dazzle
second name

the fairy of Birdsong
magic

27

Make a Wish...

Write your deepest wishes here —and doodle some dandelion fluff, just in case it helps your wishes come true.

or two... or three...

...or more

PROFILES IN DOODLING

Fill in around a shape to make a dark silhouette...

... or fill in a shape to make a white silhouette.

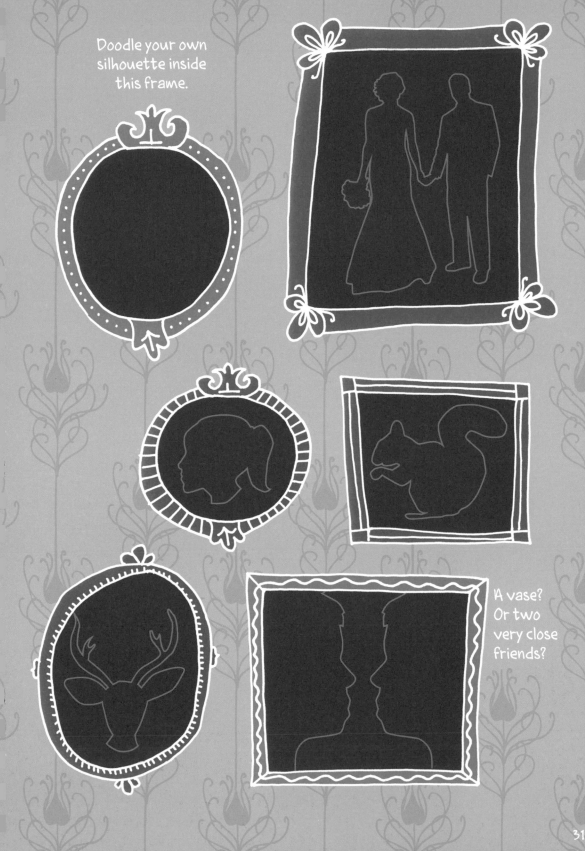

Doodle your own silhouette inside this frame.

A vase? Or two very close friends?

Life is the art of drawing without an eraser.
—John W. Gardner

Weather forecast
for tonight: Dark.
Continued dark
overnight, with
widely scattered
light by morning.
—George Carlin

ZzzZZZ* DOODLING FOR INSOMNIACS ZzzZZZZZ

THIS SONG WON'T STOP PLAYING IN MY HEAD!

TOO MUCH CAFFEINE

cola

HUNGRY

EAT ME!

What will I wear?

stupid embarrassing incident

THE FUTURE

IS THAT A SPIDER?

MUST GET UP EARLY

Draw or write what keeps you up at night. Or doodle some sheep to count.

What if

MATH TEST

zzzZZZZ

CELL OUT

If you had the biggest sign in the world,
what would it say? Fill in the cells of this digital display
to write a message everybody should see.

ABCDEFGHIJKL
MNOPQRSTUVWX
YZ0123456789

HAHA MADE YOU LOOK

JUST BE NICE

HAMSTERS ARE AWESOME

Little White Lies

Write anything you want on this page —
as long as it's not true.

Signy
♡
Broccoli!

I can believe
anything,
provided
that it
is quite
incredible.
—Oscar Wilde

We have only this moment, sparkling like a star in our hand — and melting like a snowflake.
— Marie Beynon Ray

Elsa

ME from A to Z

age:

B

best friend
forever:

cookie I'd eat
every dang day:

favorite color:

grossest food:

height:

Fill in the blanks so future students of your life will know all the important facts.

D doodle I do a lot:

e easiest subject in school:

I'm really good at:

keys I carry:

I **J** **K**

job I want someday:

47

L

last movie I saw in a theater:

M

music I listened to today:

question I would ask a talking dog:

siblings:

rating for my happiness

1	2	3	4	5
sad				stoked

Q

R

S

W

worst chore I am forced to do:

X-rays I've had:

N O P

nickname(s):

oldest stuffed
animal I own:

pets:

time I went to
bed last night:

ultimate dream
vacation:

V.I.P.* to me:

T U V

Y Z

☐ yummy
☐ yucky
black licorice

"Zoinks!"
my most frequent
exclamation:

* V.I.P. = very important person

Ladies in 18th-century France wore elaborate white wigs styled in mounds of puffs and curls. Really elegant ladies festooned their wigs with all kinds of fanciness: jewels, ships, caged birds, whatever.

What's in your cwig?

BRIGHT IDEAS

Here's a spot
to jot down all those
amazing thoughts
you're always thinking.

Need some noodling time?
Doodle doodads on these
chandeliers while you wait
for genius to strike.

BRILLIANT

Ideas are like rabbits. You get a couple and learn how to handle them, and pretty soon you have a dozen.

—John Steinbeck

Oh! the heart
is a free and a
fetterless thing,
A wave of the
ocean! a bird
on the wing!
—Julia Pardoe

The Icing on the cake

Think of three good things in your life. And then think of what makes each of them even better.

Like this —

WHO

Woof   Woof

Let the

Woof   Woof

Nogs Out!

Woof

good thing

We finally got a dog.

icing on the cake

It's Max, the best dog in the history of dogs.

good thing

icing on the cake

Doodle decorations on these yummy treats while you think of good things to write.

good thing
We Adopted
a dog

icing on the cake
We kept
the dog

good thing
I love mom

icing on the cake
Mom loves
me

Next time you need to de-stress, just start filling in every other space to make a tiled pattern. Soon you will start to feel very

calllm and **relaaaxed** and *melllow.*

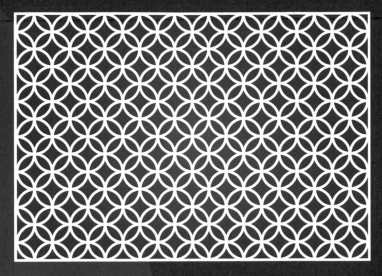

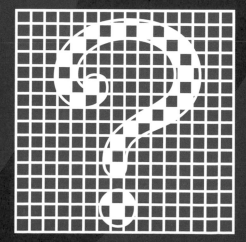

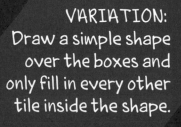

VARIATION:
Draw a simple shape
over the boxes and
only fill in every other
tile inside the shape.

The web of our life is of a mingled yarn, good and ill together.
—William Shakespeare

Art is the only way to run away without leaving home.
—Twyla Tharp

MANDALA DOODALA

Mandalas are repetitive
and restful designs — perfect
for those times when you
just want to stop worrying
and start doodling.

Let your thoughts
quiet down and
just focus on adding
details and doodads.

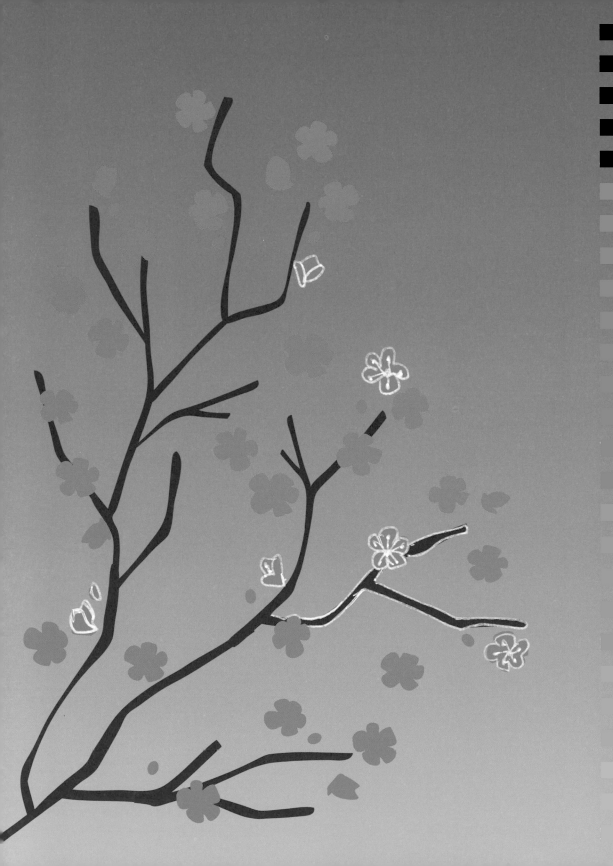

Let us be grateful to
people who make us
happy, they are the
charming gardeners
who make our
souls blossom.

— Marcel Proust

Hatred darkens life;
love illumines it.
—Martin Luther King, Jr.

If you lose the pen that came with this book, you can buy a replacement white opaque gel pen at a stationery or craft store. But that's not the only thing that can look good in this journal.

Testing

testing eeeee

Try other light, bright gel pen colors. Or light-colored pencils, pastels, or crayons.

IF IT LOOKS GOOD, KEEP ON DOODLING!

CREDITS

Art Director & Designer
Maria Corrales

Package Designer
David Avidor

Production Editor
Jen Mills

Production Coordinator
Patty Morris

Engraving on page 50 from Culver Pictures, Inc.

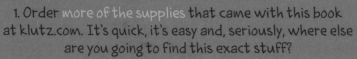

CAN'T GET ENOUGH?

Here are some simple ways
to keep the Klutz coming.

1. Order more of the supplies that came with this book at klutz.com. It's quick, it's easy and, seriously, where else are you going to find this exact stuff?

2. Get your hands on a copy of The Klutz Catalog. To request a free copy of our mail order catalog, go to klutz.com/catalog.

3. Become a Klutz Insider and get e-mail about new releases, special offers, contests, games, goofiness, and who-knows-what-all. If you're a grown-up who wants to receive e-mail from Klutz, head to klutz.com/insider.

If any of this sounds good to you, but you don't feel like going online right now, just give us a call at 1-800-737-4123. We'd love to hear from you.

more great books from KLUTZ

It's All About Me! Personality Quizzes for You and Your Friends

Doodle Journal: My Life in Scribbles

Lettering in Crazy Cool Quirky Style

Me and My Friends: The Book of Us

Sticker Design Studio

What About You?

Chalk the Block

Nail Art